Treasures of the Taylorian:
Series Three: Cultural Memory
Volume 2

Dante's Lyric Poetry in Oxford

Catalogue of the Digital Exhibition

Laura Banella, Francesco Feriozzi

Taylor Institution Library, Oxford, 2021

First published in 2021 by Taylor Institution Library

http://www.bodleian.ox.ac.uk/libraries/taylor

Dante's Lyric Poetry in Oxford. A Digital Exhibition.
https://www.cabinet.ox.ac.uk/dantes-lyric-poetry-oxford

Cover image: Dante drawing an Angel on the Anniversary of Beatrice's Death, Ashmolean Museum, https://collections.ashmolean.org/object/88790

Cover design: Emma Huber

ISBN 978-0-9954564-7-1

Taylor Institution Library, St Giles, Oxford, OX1 3NA

Preface

Laura Banella

Dante Alighieri (1265-1321) was the author of the famous *Divine Comedy*, a poem written in Tuscan vernacular. Set in the year 1300, the *Divine Comedy* tells the story of a journey through the realms of the other world: Hell, Purgatory, and Paradise. Less well known today, however, are Dante's lyric poems and treatises. His lyric production comprised more than 120 poems in diverse forms (*canzoni* and *sestine*, i.e., long lyric poems, sonnets, and ballads, written between around 1283 and 1315) as well as his *Vita Nuova* (*The New Life*). These lyric works made Dante well-known as a vernacular poet before he began writing the *Commedia*, and for two centuries they were among the most read works in Italian literature. Dante began writing the *Commedia* when he was over 40 years old, after having been a protagonist in the public life of his time and a vernacular lyric poet. His lyric poetry represents the first, fundamental stage of his literary career.

Dante gathered 31 of his poems in the *Vita Nuova* (ca. 1292-1294). The *Vita Nuova* is a *prosimetrum*: that is to say, a text made of a combination of both prose and verse. It deals with the autobiographical experience of his love for a woman named Beatrice, expressed according to a medieval courtly and philosophical understanding of lyric poetry, autobiography, and the literary genre of consolation. Dante then began to comment on some of his *canzoni* in the unfinished *Convivio* (*The Banquet*, ca. 1304-1305), but he never systematised the other ones in any organized songbook. His poems appear in manuscript volumes which usually contain other lyric poems and other texts, in collections that might or might not have been intentionally curated. During the Renaissance, Dante's lyric poems were first printed along with his *Commedia*, and later published within anthologies of early Italian poets. From the second half of the sixteenth century onwards, however, Dante did not enjoy the same success as before. The *Commedia* was still read, but he was not considered to be the most important Italian poet, and his lyric poetry was not printed throughout the whole seventeenth century. In the nineteenth century, Dante found renewed success in Italy and abroad, and along with the *Commedia*, his lyric poetry also found new publics. In the British Isles, readers, poets, and translators – such as Dante Gabriel Rossetti – were interested in Dante not just as the author of the *Commedia* but also as a poet chiefly interested in love affairs. His lyric poems were sometimes read superficially, as though they were a series of sentimental love stories, meaning that the philosophical depth of Dante's love poetry was often overlooked.

The rich holdings of Oxford libraries – the Bodleian Libraries and the Colleges' libraries – allow us to reconstruct the main channels through which Dante's lyric production has circulated from the fourteenth century to the contemporary era. The wide variety of books in the collections belonged to a diverse set of readers throughout the whole of Europe. In Oxford we can find preserved not only unique objects, but also the legacies of scholars such as Edward Moore and Paget Toynbee who studied Dante and gathered precious manuscripts and early printed editions. The Taylor Institution Library holds a rich collection of early and contemporary editions of Dante's works, including his lyric poetry. Likewise, it holds books owned by Oxonian scholars, along with materials testifying to their work as curators of Dante's *oeuvre*.

The digital exhibition and its catalogue are part of the project *LyrA - Lyric Authority: Editing and Rewriting Dante's Lyric Poetry (14th–16th c.)*, Principal Investigator Dr Laura Banella, Faculty of Medieval and Modern Languages, University of Oxford.

This project has received funding from the European Union's Horizon 2020 research and innovation programme under the Marie Skłodowska-Curie grant agreement No 892804.

Manuscripts (14th-16th century)

Laura Banella

More than 500 manuscripts of Dante's lyric poetry produced between the fourteenth and the sixteenth centuries have survived to today. They contain diverse sets of poems, from single poems to substantial and "canonized" series, often in poetic anthologies that are structured to varying degrees.

The earliest manuscripts to contain Dante's lyric poetry, his "scattered poems" (sonnets, ballads, and *canzoni* – long lyric poems) or the *Vita Nuova* (*The New Life*), were produced during the poet's life or very close to his death in 1321. The three earliest Italian *canzonieri* (anthologies of lyric poetry), compiled in Tuscany around 1300, do not devote much space to Dante and his poetic circle, the so-called *Stilnovisti* poets; instead, they focus on the poets who preceded them: the so-called Sicilian School and the Tuscans of the previous generations. Nevertheless, one of these anthologies (Florence, Biblioteca Nazionale Centrale, MS Banco Rari 217) attributes to Dante the ballad "Fresca rosa novella" ("Fresh new rose"), which other manuscripts (and most scholars) attribute to his "primo amico" ("first friend") Guido Cavalcanti. Recently, the attribution of this poem to Dante has been examined again, and some scholars believe it may indeed be authentic. If this were true, it would be the first poem by Dante to be included in a Tuscan anthology of poetry. As for Northern Italian manuscripts, the famous *canzoniere Escorialense* (Real Biblioteca de San Lorenzo de El Escorial, MS lat. e III 23), compiled in Padua between ca. 1290 and 1315, contains some of Dante's sonnets and ballads. Among these are earlier versions of some of the poems of the *Vita Nuova*. Finally, the book owned and partially written by Niccolò de' Rossi, a poet from Treviso in the Veneto region, includes many of Dante's poems in a diverse literary anthology that was most probably completed by 1335 (Vatican City, Biblioteca Apostolica Vaticana, MS Barb. Lat. 3953). The earliest complete copy of the *Vita Nuova* (Florence, Biblioteca Medicea Laurenziana, MS Martelli 12) was copied in the first quarter of the fourteenth century, probably in Gubbio, in Umbria (central Italy), before being brought to Florence. These books testify to Dante's success as a lyric poet before he became the celebrated poet-theologian of the *Commedia*, as well as to the early circulation of his lyrics beyond Florence and Tuscany. Thus they bring to light the precocious interest in Dante and in Tuscan poetry that existed in Venice and on the Venetian *terraferma* (mainland). During the fourteenth and fifteenth centuries, Dante's lyric poetry circulated widely throughout the whole of Italy: we have hundreds of manuscripts dating from this period. His poems were printed for the first time in 1491, as an appendix to a Venetian reprint of the *Commedia* with Cristoforo Landino's commentary. As for many of Dante's literary works, their manuscript circulation certainly did not end at the moment they were printed: still today, we have many manuscripts of Dante's lyric poems that were produced during the Renaissance, in the sixteenth century as well as the seventeenth.

The Bodleian Libraries do not hold any of the earliest copies of Dante's lyric poetry. Yet the manuscripts of his poems, of the *Vita Nuova*, and of the *Convivio* in Oxford today are important examples of the kinds of manuscripts preserving Dante's lyric production that were created from the late fourteenth century to the first half of the sixteenth. Some are paper manuscripts compiled by middle-class readers; others are lavishly illuminated parchment codices commissioned by the elites. What is more, they represent the two focal centres of Dante's reception: Florence and Venice. This exhibition encompasses volumes from Florence, where Dante remained – along with Petrarch – a recognised cultural authority, as well as northern Italian codices (some specifically recognizable as having been produced in Venice), where the relationship with Dante appears to have been more nuanced. In northern Italy, Dante struggled to be recognised as an authority; rather, from as early as the last decades of the fourteenth century it was Petrarch who assumed a predominant role.

Manuscripts (14th-16th century)

The most ancient manuscript with Dante's lyric poetry preserved at the Bodleian Library does not contain any poem today confirmed as authentic. MS Can. Ital. 111 (n° 11) was compiled between the end of the fourteenth and the beginning of the fifteenth century in Venice, by a Giovanni de' Garzoni. It then passed through different hands and in the fifteenth century probably arrived in the nearby city of Padua, the location of a prestigious university. It is one of the few manuscripts in which the *Commedia* is accompanied by a collection of lyric poetry. In fact, of the hundreds of manuscripts of Dante's lyric poetry and of his *Commedia*, less than a dozen contain both of these. In this manuscript, Dante appears as friend and correspondent of Giovanni Quirini (Venice, before 1295-1333), the most famous poet in early fourteenth-century Venice. Quirini's connection to Dante has a long-standing tradition, emerging earlier than 1382, when in Giovanni Girolamo Nadal's *Leandreride*, a poem narrating the myth of Hero and Leander, Dante's character makes a list of contemporary poets which starts with him, saying: "il primo è Ian Querin, che mi fu amico/ in vita" ("the first one is Ian Querin [Giovanni Quirini], who was a friend of mine / in life"). The actual friendship between Dante and Quirini has been denied, as has the authenticity of the exchanges in sonnets between the two. It is true, however, that Quirini had a deep interest in Dante's poetry. In one of his most famous sonnets, he writes to a noble lord, who is to be identified with Cangrande della Scala, nobleman ruler of Verona and host to Dante in the 1310s, asking him to disclose Dante's *Paradiso*: supposedly he had received a copy of *Paradiso* but did not make it public and thus others were not able to read and copy it. In another sonnet, serving as accompanying note, Quirini writes to a friend that he is sending delayed his own copy of the *Commedia* because of an illness; there, he also pleads with the recipient to keep the book safe and to return it as soon as possible. This volume could well be the first copy of the *Commedia* circulating in Venice. The only poem of MS Can. Ital. 111 (and more generally of these exchanges between Quirini and a friend that some manuscripts name as Dante) that today is attributed – albeit doubtfully – by some scholars to Alighieri is the sonnet "Nulla mi parve mai più crudel cosa" ("Nothing appeared to me as more cruel"). It is a good quality poem, yet its inclusion in the canon seems to be due more to its twentieth-century success than to the historical possibility that it had actually been sent by Dante to Giovanni Quirini. Indeed, Eugenio Montale (1896-1981, 1975 Nobel Prize in Literature) quotes two verses of this sonnet in his poem "La primavera hitleriana" ("The Hitler Spring," dated 1939-1946), a poem written in relation to a significant historical event: "Hitler and Mussolini in Florence. Evening gala at the Teatro Comunale. Over the Arno, a snow of white butterflies" (note by the author; the meeting took place on May 9, 1938). Line 9 of the medieval sonnet serves as an exergue, along with the mention of Giovanni Quirini as the addressee ("*Né quella ch'a veder lo sol si gira* ... | -Dante (?) to Giovanni Quirini"), while line 10 is incorporated within the text itself with only light modifications: "Clizia, ... tu | che il non mutato amor mutata serbi." ("Clizia, ... | changed one harboring changeless love.") What is more, this is the first mention of Clizia, a figure of poetry of major importance for Montale. The sonnet, therefore, influenced Montale when it came to a crucial component of his lyric production. Likely in part for this reason, it seems to have earned its inclusion in the corpus of Dante, and thus its "canonization" among one of the most influential lyric corpora of Italian literary history, notwithstanding its real authorship.

The renowned Italian writer Giovanni Boccaccio (1313-1375), author of the *Decameron*, compiled an extremely successful edition of Dante's works. In the 1350s-1360s he copied in his own hand three volumes containing fifteen of Dante's *canzoni* (long lyric poems) and the *Commedia*; two of them also contain the *Vita Nuova*; one of them pairs Dante's works with Petrarch's lyric collection, the *Canzoniere*. In each of these books, a *Life of Dante* written by Boccaccio introduces the works. The three volumes were in turn copied and imitated, thus generating a tradition of volumes that reproduced the editorial choices made by Boccaccio for Dante's works.

One of the manuscripts encompassed in the exhibition derives from these Dantean anthologies by Boccaccio. MS Can. Ital. 114 (n° 9) was copied in the second half of the fifteenth century by Filippo Benci for his family's library. It contains Dante's *Vita Nuova*, *canzoni*, and the *Convivio*. The *Convivio*, Dante's unfinished philosophical treatise, was not included by Boccaccio in his edition of Dante's works. However, after limited circulation in the fourteenth century and the first half of the fifteenth, in the second half of the fifteenth century the treatise enjoyed renewed success and, in Medici-ruled Florence, it circulated among different social classes. We have sumptuous manuscripts owned by the richest families, some commissioned by the Medici family: the best instance of these is an illuminated volume made of parchment containing a collection of Dante's works (*Vita Nuova*, *canzoni*, and *Convivio*, along with poems by the Tuscan poet Bonaccorso da Montemagno), gifted by Lorenzo de' Medici to the Aragonese, the ruling family of the Kingdom of Naples (Florence, Società Dantesca Italiana, MS 3, 1468?). And we have many extant far less pretentious copies, read and sometimes copied by the Florentine bourgeoisie, such as the aforementioned volume by Filippo Benci.

Produced in the same cultural environment and roughly contemporary, MS Can. Ital. 99 (n° 6) bears the Medici coat of arms and pairs Dante's lyric poetry with Lorenzo de Medici's and Angelo Poliziano's lyric poems, thus embodying Dante's role as the most illustrious antecedent of contemporary Florentine literature (see below).

The Bodleian codices coming from the Veneto region represent very well the diverse types of books we have today of Dante's lyric poetry. As we have seen above, MS Can. Ital. 111 was compiled personally by a Venetian named Giovanni de' Garzoni, who copied in a merchant cursive script. Even though he used second-hand parchment (the book is a palimpsest, i.e., the texts have been superimposed on earlier, effaced writing), he might have been one of the many wealthy Venetian merchants, and possibly one of the Garzoni who entered the Great Council of Venice – the political organ of the Republic composed of patrician families – following the War of Chioggia (1378-1381). Other wealthy families commissioned professional scribes to write their books and had them lavishly decorated. An example is MS Can. Ital. 70 (n° 4), a copy of

Petrarch's vernacular poetry which attributes to Dante a sonnet on the nature of love: it was compiled in northern Italy, possibly in Ferrara, in the second half of the fifteenth century, and was most probably commissioned from a professional scribe and richly illuminated. MS Can. Ital. 81 pairs Dante and Petrarch with a local poet, Jacopo Sanguinacci. Just as we have seen before for Florence, by placing Sanguinacci's poetry together with Petrarch's and Dante's vernacular poetry, this book demonstrates a desire to "canonize" the contemporary, local Venetian poetic production in relation to the two most important poets of the time. The anthologies adding local writers to the historical ones show the same perspective as Nadal's parade of poets in his *Leandreride*, which ends with Venetian poets alongside the major glories of vernacular poetry.

MS Can. Ital. 101 (n° 7) exemplifies the manuscript circulation of literature during the sixteenth century. The manuscript medium was in fact used even long after the age of printing had begun. Compiled when Dante's lyric poems had already been printed at least once, in 1491, this book demonstrates the persistence of handwritten volumes in the age of print, both as a necessity when it came to works that were not widely available in printed format, and as a choice for particular literary genres. Indeed, printed editions of Dante's lyric poetry were not common until the nineteenth century, while lyric poetry was one of the genres that circulated widely in manuscripts during the Renaissance.

Finally, the exhibition includes a codex that was copied in particular circumstances: the nobleman and politician Antonio de' Petrucci from Siena compiled MS Can. Ital. 50 (n° 2) when he was held in prison in Urbino in 1464. Here, Dante's lyric poetry is included in a miscellany that combines moral sayings attributed to various authors with some short texts by Antonio himself, together with a substantial anthology of vernacular poetry. It is not a luxury book, but Andrea de' Petrucci copied tidily and used quality materials; he also rubricated and decorated his book, albeit in a rather basic way. During the Middle Ages, many manuscripts were produced in prison and Andrea's volume is an example of books which were compiled by privileged inmates who were able to copy and write to ease the unpleasantness of the time they spent incarcerated.

Bodleian Library, MS Can. Ital. 70, f. 1r (Digital Bodleian)

The Manuscripts of Dante's Lyric Poetry at the Bodleian Library

1. A Copy of the *Convivio*

Oxford, Bodleian Library, MS Ital. d. 5

Tuscany? 1463

Paper; ff. 113; mm 288 x 198; prose and verses copied in a single column, in a humanistic minuscule by one hand. Some marginal corrections and notes, probably by the scribe. On f. 45*v* a note and a *manicula* (pointing hand) by another 15th c. hand. Stains and sketchy pen drawings on some pages (by a child?). On f. 1*v*, two notes on P. Bonaparte, the second one by E. Moore. One page is missing between pp. 38 and 39, and two between pp. 109 and 110.

For the start of the *Convivio*, f. 2*r*, a 8-line ornamental initial [*S*] in gold on a ground of blue, red, and green, with white highlighting, and white vine-stem interlace (*bianchi girari*); in the lower margin, a matching border with white vine-stem interlace (*bianchi girari*) on a shaped ground of blue, red, and green with white higlighting, with central space in a wreath for a coat of arms. For the *canzoni*, 4-5-line plain initials in blue; for the book divisions, 3-4-line plain initials blue (missing for books 1 and 2); for all other chapter divisions, plain initials in red in the margin adjacent to the text. Some rubrics, in red (from ch. I 6, irregular).

Antique parchment binding.

[Central Italy: Tuscany?]; Pierantonio di Benedetto Buonaparte (Florence, 16th c.); Bocca Bookshop in Rome (19th c.); E. Moore (Oxford, from June 1880); Bodleian Library (from 1916).

The manuscript contains only Dante's *Convivio*. Colophon on f. 111*r*: "Fine alla terça cançona di maggo a di 18 1463" ("End at the third song in may on the 18th day 1463"). On f. 2*r*, a different hand from the scribe, writes: "Convivio di Dante Alighieri fiorentino di Pierantonio di Benedetto

Buonaparte e delli amici parenti e di tutti quelli che se ne volessino servire" ("Convivio by the Florentine Dante Alighieri of Pierantonio di Benedetto Buonaparte and of his friends family and of anyone who would use it"). This same hand probably added the Bonaparte coat of arms in the lower margin.

The manuscript is an example of the renewed interest in the *Convivio* in the second half of the fifteenth century when, in Florence particularly, Dante's unfinished treatise captured the attention of Lorenzo de' Medici and his intellectual circle. Like many codices of Dante's minor works of this period, it is made of paper. It is not a luxury book, but its fairly good-quality decoration and the regular script point toward an upper-class readership.

2. A Miscellany Written in Prison

Oxford, Bodleian Library, MS Can. Ital. 50

Italy, Urbino; 1464; Antonio de' Petrucci from Siena

Paper; ff. IV+236+III'; mm 219x143; verses copied in a single column, prose copied in full page; cursive script by Antonio de' Petrucci. Pen-flourished initials for some of the poems. Some rubrics in red. Some brackets and *maniculae* by the scribe.

Binding in cardboard and leather.

Italy, Urbino; Matteo Luigi Canonici, 1727–1805; Giuseppe Canonici, -1807; at the Bodleian Library since 1817.

The volume contains miscellaneous texts: Augustine's Latin letters; moral sayings attributed to Seneca, Dante, Valerius Maximus, Petrarch; a quite substantial anthology of vernacular poems (by Petrarch, Dante, Malatesta da Pesaro, Simone Serdini, Antonio da Ferrara, Alberto Orlando da Fabriano, Leonardo Bruni, Tommaso da Rieti, Sennuccio del Bene, Giusto de' Conti, Giudantonio da Urbino, Angelo Galli da Urbino, and anonymous); and some of Andrea de' Petrucci's own letters and other short texts. Andrea signs the book three times: «Ex arce urbini die xxvi° augusti 1464 manu propria»

(f. 7*r*); «Qui liber scriptus est et finitus fuir a me Antonio de petrucciis de Sena, milite, ac paterni comite, in arce urbini et in eadem carcerato sub annis d(omi)ni 1464 die xxv inuij» (f. 231*r*); «Ex Arce urbini die x° nouembris 1464» (f. 236*v*).

Andrea de' Petrucci (Siena, 1400–Forlì, 1471) belonged to one of the richest and most powerful families in Siena; he was a leading politician whose influence went beyond his motherland. He is the only Sienese leader mentioned by contemporary historians and chroniclers: cited for instance by Pope Pius II Piccolomini and Niccolò Machiavelli. He was imprisoned by Federico di Montefeltro in Urbino in October 1461 and remained there until October 1465. While incarcerated, he compiled this miscellany with texts he found in the Montefeltro library. Dante's lyric poems here are divided into two sections: a large, cohesive series that encompasses some poems from the *Vita Nuova* and sixteen *canzoni*, introduced in the rubric as "moral poems" (f. 10r); and two spurious sonnets, entitled "devotissimi di Dante" (f. 73v, "most pious by Dante").

3. Sonnets by Dante in a Lyric Miscellany

Oxford, Bodleian Library, MS Can. Ital. 65

Italy; 15th century, third quarter.

Paper; ff. I+138+I'; mm 282x132; verses copied in a single column; copied by one hand in a cursive humanistic script; some red rubrics and initials.

Leather binding with gold decoration.

Italy; Matteo Luigi Canonici, 1727–1805; Giuseppe Canonici, -1807. Purchased by the Bodleian in 1817.

The MS contains: Petrarch's *Canzoniere* including additional *disperse* (i.e., extravagant poems); forty-four poems (mainly sonnets) by different authors, including Boccaccio, Dante, Sennuccio del Bene, and Petrarch (most of these poems are anonymous); alphabetical index of the first lines of the *Canzoniere* poems; Petrarch's *Triumphs*.

In this unadorned manuscript, Petrarch's *Canzoniere* is followed by an anthology of poems by various authors, among which only some bear an attribution. There are three sonnets by Dante intermingled with these lyric poems, two of which are anonymous: "Spesse fiate me vien a la mente," with the rubric "De Dante" ("by Dante," f. 103*r*); "Due donne in cima de la mente mia;" "Tanto gentile et tanto honesta pare."

The oblong shape of this codex is not common, but is not unique: other contemporary copies of Dante's lyric poetry share the form of MS Can. Ital. 65 (MSS Strasbourg, Bibliothèque nationale et universitaire, 1808 (L. It. 7); Florence, Società Dantesca Italiana, 3). When opened, the page spread of oblong books is squared or almost squared. This shape was common in medieval merchant account-books.

4. Petrarch's *Canzoniere* and *Triumphs* with one sonnet attributed to Dante

Oxford, Bodleian Library, MS Can. Ital. 70

Italy [North East/Ferrara]; 15th century, third quarter.

Parchment; ff. II+202+III'; mm 242x155; verses copied in a single column, prose in full-page layout; copied by one hand in humanistic script; different types of painted and decorated initials, titles in gold, rubrics and some relevant words in red.

For the start of the *Canzoniere* (f. 3*r*), surround border with white vine-stem interlace (*bianchi girari*). Initial [*V*] in red on a ground of blue and gold, with portrait of author holding a book. In the border, one roundel containing Laura and another featuring an emblem of a padlocked book; also two lozenges with knotwork decoration. Painted initials in gold. For the start of the *Triumphs* (f. 144*r*), gold initial [*N*] with vine-stem interlace (*bianchi girari*) in a gold frame. Multi-coloured leaf extensions, gold filigree penwork, and gold balls. Painted initials with gold also at ff. 101*v*, 156*v*,

160*r*, 169*v*, 176*v*, 179*r*. Minor initials in colour (red or blue).

Red leather binding.

Italy, Ferrara?; Matteo Luigi Canonici, 1727–1805; Giuseppe Canonici, -1807. Purchased by the Bodleian in 1817.

The MS contains: Petrarch's *Canzoniere* and *Triumphs*; the note on Laura's death; Sicco Polenton's *Life of Petrarch*; pseudo-Antonio da Tempo's commentary on *Canzoniere* 1; other short texts, which include one sonnet probably by Dante.

This lavishly illuminated copy of Petrarch's vernacular poetry belongs to a group of manuscripts that entitle his *Canzoniere* "Carmen Rithimonos Elegicum," thus emphasizing its elegiac qualities. This manuscript, along with the MS Reg. lat. 1110 held at the Biblioteca Apostolica Vaticana, also contains one sonnet attributed to Dante, "Molti volendo dir che fosse amore" ("Many wanting to say what love is"), which deals with the nature of love and its phenomenology. The inclusion of this sonnet stresses to us the ways in which, in this group of codices, the role of Petrarch is specifically that of a love poet. The scribe of this codex copied two other copies of Petrarch's vernacular works: London, British Library, MS Harley 3442; and Oxford, Bodleian Library, MS Can. Ital. 76.

5. A Poetic Anthology from the Veneto

Oxford, Bodleian Library, MS Can. Ital. 81

Italy, Venice or Padua; 15th century.

Paper; mm 2058x137; ff. II+176+I', with original numbering; written by one hand in a merchant cursive script; verses copied in a single column; rubrics in violet. Pen-flourished initials, alternately in blue and red with violet decoration.

On f. iii*v*, a full-page drawing of a pine tree, with the Morosini coat of arms (18th century?).

Matteo Luigi Canonici, 1727–1805; Giuseppe Canonici, -1807. Purchased by the Bodleian in 1817

The codex contains a selection of poems from Petrarch's *Canzoniere* (80 sonnets, then *canzoni* and *sestine*), entitled "Flores sonetorum Petrarce;" a series of *canzoni* by Dante (9 poems), Simone Serdini, and Jacopo Sanguinacci.

This paper manuscript pairs a minor poet from Padua, Jacopo Sanguinacci, with one of the most successful poets of the fifteenth century in Italy, Simone Serdini, and with the two poetic authorities of the time, Petrarch and Dante. This selection locates the manuscript in the Veneto and testifies to the success in this area of Petrarch, whose poems where sometimes followed by some by Dante.

6. A Florentine Poetic Anthology

Oxford, Bodleian Library, MS Can. Ital. 99

Italy, Tuscany/Florence; 15th century *exeunte*.

Paper; mm 210x140; ff. II+179; verses written in one single column in a humanistic minuscule. Coloured initials in red and blue. For the beginning of Dante's *canzoni* (long lyric poems) series, a golden initial [*D*] on a ground of blue and red; painted multi-coloured leaf border with gold balls on the left, superior, and inferior margin. Medici coat of arms, held by two naked *putti*, in the *bas de page*. Title rubric in gold on a ground of red.

Red leather binding with gold decoration.

Italy, Florence; Matteo Luigi Canonici, 1727–1805; Giuseppe Canonici, -1807. Purchased by the Bodleian in 1817.

The codex contains poems by Dante, Lorenzo de' Medici, Angelo Poliziano, Petrarch, Antonio Tebaldeo, and others.

This poetic anthology is opened by a series of nineteen of Dante's *canzoni* (long lyric poems) and ballads. It pairs Dante's lyric poetry with poems by Lorenzo de' Medici, Angelo Poliziano (*rispetti*), Petrarch (a sonnet), Tebaldeo (an eclogue), and others. It testifies to the success and the authoritative role attributed to Dante in late fifteenth-century Florence - for his *Commedia* but also for his so-called 'minor' works - when the Medici appropriated the illustrious Florentine vernacular literature, and especially Dante, to support their cultural and political influence. The most famous example is the *Raccolta Aragonese*: this collection of Tuscan early and contemporary vernacular lyric poetry was prepared by Poliziano and Lorenzo de' Medici – with Lorenzo adding his own poetry - to send to Federico of Aragon, the younger son of the King of Naples.

7. A Reinassance Manuscript of Dante's Lyric Poetry

Oxford, Bodleian Library, MS Can. Ital. 101 (unit II)

Italy, 16th century

Paper; ff. 48 + I; mm 206 x 150 (this codex is bound with a 15th-century copy of Giovanni Boccaccio's *Ninfale fiesolano*); verses copied in a single column in a cursive script by two hands (the first hand only copies ff. 62*v*-64*v*, a quire probably added later; the second, principal hand is probably earlier). Copious marginal variant readings in the pages copied by the second hand, by this same scribe, derived from the source used for the text (M. Barbi, *Studi sul Canzoniere di Dante*, Firenze, Sansoni, 1915, 23-26). Some other marginal annotations by a much later hand.

Rubrics in brown ink.

18th-century binding, cardboard and leather.

Italy; Matteo Luigi Canonici, 1727–1805; Giuseppe Canonici, -1807; Bodleian Library (from 1817).

The manuscript contains two series of poems by Dante. One has just five poems, and precedes the other, written earlier and made up of 21 poems.

Some of the texts are spurious.

This simple volume is an example of the late manuscript circulation of Dante's lyric poetry. Compiled when Dante's poems had already been printed at least once, it demonstrates the persistence of the manuscript medium well into the age of printing. Printed editions of Dante's lyric poetry were not common, and lyric poetry was one of the genres that circulated widely in manuscripts during the Renaissance. What is more, the first printed edition of Dante's lyric poems (1491) was an appendix to a large, commented *Commedia*, while lyric poetry circulated in small books, both manuscripts and printed editions, which could be held in one hand. This was the format chosen by Aldo Manuzio for his editions of the Classics, as well as for both Dante's *Commedia* (1502) and Petrarch's *Canzoniere* (1501).

8. A *Commedia* with a Lyric Collection

Oxford, Bodleian Library, MS Can. Ital. 111

Italy, Venice; 14th century *exeunte* – 15th century *ineunte*; Giovanni de' Garzoni; Biagio da Ragusa.

Parchment, palimpsest (the earlier text is an unidentified Latin work); mm 345x230; ff. 158. Written by two principal hands: Giovanni de' Garzoni, in a merchant cursive script (ff. 1-141*r*; 152-155, 156*v*); Biagio da Ragusa, cursive humanistic script (ff. 141*v*-151*v*). Different layouts mirroring the different phases of copy. Some rubrics in red.

Binding in parchment and cardboard.

Italy, Venice and Veneto, 15th century; Matteo Luigi Canonici, 1727–1805; Giuseppe Canonici, -1807; purchased by the Bodleian in 1817.

The volume contains a lyric anthology with poems by Zianin de' Garzoni (?), Giovanni Quirini, Antonio da Ferrara, Petrarch, Dante (?), Ventura Monachi, Giovanni Frescobaldi, Guglielmotto d'Otranto, Domenico da

Montecchiello, and anonymous (ff. 1-19); Dante's *Commedia* (ending at *Par.* 31.123, ff. 20-151); Graziolo Bambaglioli's *Trattato delle virtù morali* (ff. 152-155).

Various ownership notes: f. 1*v* "Zianin de Garzoni" and "de Nichollo T(re)vixan de mis(er) ioachi(n) d(e) sanlucha. Cho(m)pra in piaza a i(n)chanto da s(er) Andrea d(e) ma[risc]cha[...]ch[.]o a di vi zener 1411 [the last two numbers written on 02] per ducati 9, d., 15, s. 27», a signature *Zuane grigo*; f. 141*r*, at the end of *Purgatorio*: «Mccccxxxxv die septima noue(m)br(is). Explicit purgatorius liber p(er) blasium raguxe(um) qui stetit in domo d(omi)ni pauli lauredano adlaude(m) dej scriptor scripsisset 7 mellius si ualuisset: certe»; f. 158*v*: «Jachob de zudio scripsisset» «De padova [...] 1456 xd 10 maxi» (this note suggests that the manuscripts arrived in Padua).

This incomplete copy of the *Commedia* is preceded by a poetic anthology, with poems attributed spuriously to Dante. Copied in Venice in the late fourteenth century by Giovanni de' Garzoni, possibly a member of a naturalized Florentine family, it was later completed by Biagio da Ragusa in the house of the Loredan family. The poetic anthology has been compiled in five different phases, and the poems have been written with varying layouts, according to what space was left. Three poems are attributed to Dante: "Tolete via le vostre porte omai" (f. 16*v*, «da(n)tte | Amo(r) Cogitaciones Spes Virttus et Racio», sonnet by Quirini), and two of the correspondence sonnets between Dante and the Venetian poet Giovanni Quirini: "Se 'l primo huomo se fosse difeso" (c. 10*r*[b], «r° dantis»); "Con plu sospiri avanti costei vegno" (c. 10*v*[b], «r° dantis»); the third, "Nulla mi parve mai più crudel cosa" (f. 19*r*[b]) here is anonymous. By portraying Dante as a friend of Quirini, as in Giovanni Girolamo Nadal's *Leandreride*, this manuscript establishes a connection between the poet of the *Commedia* and the city of Venice.

9. An Anthology of Dante's 'Minor' Works

Oxford, Bodleian Library, MS Can. Ital. 114

Italy, Florence; 15th century, before 1475; Filippo Benci.

Paper; mm 195x287; ff. II+196, written in a merchant cursive script by Filippo Benci. Verses written in one single column, prose in full-page layout. Red rubrics. Pen-flourished initials for the beginning of the texts, and some coloured initials in red.

Italy, Florence; Matteo Luigi Canonici, 1727–1805; Giuseppe Canonici , -1807. Purchased by the Bodleian Library in 1817.

The manuscript contains the *Vita Nuova*, a series of Dante's lyric poems, and the *Convivio*.

Filippo Benci was a member of a Florentine family of *linaioli*, linen workers, who in the fifteenth century owned a considerable library consisting of simple yet thoroughly copied or commissioned volumes, like this 'Dantean anthology' encompassing *Vita Nuova* (*The New Life*), lyric poems, and *Convivio*. This manuscript derives from Boccaccio's fourteenth-century edition of Dante's works, but adds the *Convivio* and some lyrics to the selection while excluding the *Commedia* (of which the Benci family owned other copies). Filippo's brothers were part of the Florentine cultural élite: Tommaso and Giovanni Benci were called *comphilosophi* by Marsilius Ficinus, who in 1463 asked Tommaso Benci to translate his *Pimander* into the vernacular. Their grandfather, Giovanni di Taddeo Benci, was a friend of the famous humanist Coluccio Salutati.

Early Printed Editions (1491-1727)

Francesco Feriozzi

Historical background

From the the late fifteenth century to the early sixteenth century, the Italian peninsula remained just as divided as it had been throughout the middle ages, its many separate states dominated by noble families and in constant war with one another. Gradually, Spain and France increased their influence on Italy, limiting the independence of the individual states but never managing to impose any form of political unification. Nevertheless, despite these political divisions and despite the lack of a common language (each region having its own vernacular language), it was during these years that an Italian literary canon, based on Tuscan literature and thus language, took shape.

The construction of the canon was the consequence of a new attention paid to vernacular poetry. Largely neglected by the early humanists, this poetry finally achieved equal consideration with Latin literature at the turn of the sixteenth century. From that point on, the literary tradition of the vernacular was investigated with unprecedented rigour, while political powers and intellectual authorities used this newfound interest to push their agendas through their editions. The development of the printing industry, meanwhile, allowed literary works – new ones and classics alike – to reach an unprecedented level of diffusion, thus offering an effective means of disseminating the canon.

The most popular vernacular author throughout the century was undeniably Petrarch, who became the main model for lyric poetry throughout Italy and much of Europe. Dante's lyric production received less attention, and was either included in wider anthologies or relegated to the appendices of other works. Nevertheless, the Renaissance editions of his lyric works are extremely interesting: not only for understanding the perception of Dante as a lyric poet in the Renaissance, but also as instruments in a "cultural war" between

Florence, hometown of the poet, and Venice, a rising economic power that attempted to appropriate Tuscany's literary heritage.

Dante between Venice and Florence

In early Renaissance manuscripts, Dante's lyric poetry is often associated with the works of the other major fourteenth-century Tuscan poet, Petrarch (cf. the Manuscripts section). The rest of the canon, meanwhile, tends to vary depending on where the manuscript was produced. Two of the fifteenth-century manuscripts shown in this exhibition (MSS Can. Ital. 99 and Can. Ital. 81) are a good example of the rise of conflicting canons in different parts of Italy. The first of these, produced in Tuscany and connected with the Medici family, is unashamedly Florence-centric, placing Dante and Petrarch beside the fifteenth-century authors Lorenzo de' Medici and Angelo Poliziano. The second was produced not in Tuscany but in the Veneto, and includes Dante, Petrarch, the Tuscan Simone Serdini (who died in the first quarter of the fifteenth century and was extremely successful at the time), and Jacopo Sanguinacci, a minor poet from Padua, near Venice. Therefore, while they both agree on the Florentine roots of their canons, the two manuscripts diverge when it comes to the fifteenth century: while the Tuscan one presents an uninterrupted continuity from Dante and Petrarch to fifteenth-century Florentine poets, the other mostly ignores fifteenth-century Tuscan poetry in favour of the Veneto's own production.

For most of the Renaissance, Florence carried out a campaign of 'cultural reappropriation' of Dante. Before dying in his exile, Dante had written well-known invectives against his native city in the *Commedia*. Afterwards, however, Florentine intellectuals strove to present him as a Florentine national glory. The common conception of Dante as ill-tempered is in part connected with the Florentines' attempt to present his invectives as his excesses, rather than as the consequence of how the city treated him. Part of this process of reappropriation was the rediscovery of Dante's lyric production, included in 1476-77 in a manuscript collection of Tuscan verse from fourteenth-century and contemporary authors curated by Angelo Poliziano on behalf of Lorenzo de' Medici and donated to Frederick of Aragon. Known as the *Raccolta aragonese* ("Aragonese collection"), this collection was part of a cultural operation led by the Medici to construct a Tuscan poetic canon from the middle ages to their own era, and to project cultural authority as a mirror for political power.

This attitude can also be seen in Cristoforo Landino's commentary to the *Commedia*. First printed in 1481 in Florence itself, this commentary soon came to be considered as a crucial instrument to the understanding of Dante's major poem, both inside and outside of Italy. On display here are two copies of a 1491 reprint of the *Commedia* with Landino's commentary (n° 1), one of which belonged to a Spanish reader, testifying to the European popularity of the poem. This edition is accompanied by an index to ease navigation within the commentary. It also features woodcuts – an impressive testament to the craft of Venetian woodcutters – inspired by the illuminations found in manuscript copies of the *Commedia*. Moreover, the edition includes eighteen lyric poems by Dante: this marks the first time that these poems were ever printed, and hence is the sign of an early interest for Dante's lyric production.

A cultural conflict

The fact that the 1491 *Commedia* is one of several editions printed in Venice is particularly significant. The city was indeed on the rise as the most important centre for the printing industry in the peninsula. It was in Venice that Aldo Manuzio printed (in 1501 and 1502 respectively) the most important editions of Petrarch's *Fragmenta* and of Dante's *Commedia* to be produced during the sixteenth century. Among the many reasons why these editions stand out is the extraordinary philological care that their editor Pietro Bembo employed in establishing the texts, reconstructing their pure Tuscan form. In 1514, Manuzio put out another edition of Petrarch's *Fragmenta*, which – significantly – included an appendix of medieval poems by various authors (n° 2). Among these are the three Tuscan poems cited in Petrarch's poem "Lasso me" ("Ah me"), including one by Dante ("Così nel mio parlar vogli'esser aspro," "I want to be so harsh in my speech"). The Venetians were also the first to publish Dante's lyric verse within a printed anthology: the collection known as *Canzoni di Dante* ("Songs by Dante," 1518), of which there is no copy in Oxford. It is clear from these examples that Venetians were attempting to 'appropriate' the Tuscan literary tradition.

The latent conflict between the Venetians and the Tuscans over the Florentine literary heritage spilled over into open war after 1525, when the aforementioned Pietro Bembo published a dialogue titled *Prose* (*Proses*). In this dialogue, Bembo explicitly proposed Petrarch and Boccaccio as linguistic models for anyone aiming to write in the vernacular. Dante, despite being mentioned in multiple passages of the dialogue, is often reprimanded, mainly for his mixing of different stylistic levels in the *Commedia*. By proposing Petrarch and Boccaccio as exclusive models, Bembo effectively effaced the rest of the medieval tradition and ignored the entirety of fifteenth-century Tuscan production, while at the same time 'eradicating' these authors from Florence. Famously, he went as far as to claim that writing in the vernacular was easier for a non-Tuscan than for a Tuscan, on the basis that the latter risked involuntarily tarnishing the language with the uncouth, modern Tuscan.

The *Prose* were obviously seen by the Florentines as a direct attack on their literary tradition. Their response to this came in 1527 in the form of a collection entitled *Sonetti e canzoni di diversi antichi autori toscani* (*Sonnets and songs by multiple ancient Tuscan authors*, on display, n° 3), better known as the 'Giuntina di rime antiche' ("Giuntina of ancient rhymes," from the name of its printer, Bernardo di Giunta). The 'Giuntina', partially based on the *Raccolta Aragonese*, is an impressive collection of 289 medieval Tuscan poems arranged over eleven books. It was edited by a group of learned Florentines with the intention of showing that the Tuscan canon was in fact much larger than Bembo's limited presentation. Significantly, the first four books are entirely devoted to Dante, while Petrarch is entirely absent. Regardless of its 'political agenda', the 'Giuntina' provided an extremely rich collection of medieval verse, and it was reprinted with minor changes in Venice itself by Antonio da Sabbio in 1532 (on display, n° 4).

Dante's other works

Dante included lyric poems in his two "minor" vernacular works, the *Vita nuova* (*The New Life*) and the *Convivio* (*The Banquet*). While both were widely known to sixteenth-century intellectuals, both went through significantly fewer printed editions than Dante's *Commedia*, and mostly circulated in manuscript form.

The *Vita nuova* is one of Dante's earliest works. It is a loosely autobiographical history of Dante's love for Beatrice through a mixture of prose and poetry. Despite its fundamental importance for understanding much of the *Commedia*'s allegorical and historical background, it was only printed once during the Renaissance, in 1576 (on display, n° 6). In this proudly Florentine edition by the editor Sermartelli, the text was accompanied by fifteen *canzoni* and Boccaccio's celebratory *Life of Dante*. Before being printed, however, the *Vita Nuova* enjoyed a good diffusion via manuscripts, as attested by the late-15th century Florentine anthology displayed here, which contains the *Vita Nuova* in addition to the *Convivio* and some poems (Can. Ital. 114).

The *Convivio*, written by Dante shortly after his exile, is a philosophical-didactic work built entirely around prose commentaries to lyric poems by Dante himself. The work remained unfinished and seems to have had little to no circulation between Dante's abandonment of the project and the 1440s, when it was undoubtedly known to intellectuals connected with Florence such as Lorenzo de' Medici, Angelo Poliziano, and Cristoforo Landino. The *Convivio* was first printed in Florence in 1490, but all subsequent editions over the course of the following century came from the Venetian printing industry, as is the case for the 1531 copy on display here, which belonged to John Donne (n° 5).

Italy around 1494

(from Wikipedia)

Early Printed Editions of Dante's Lyric Poetry in Oxford Libraries

1. Dante Alighieri, *La Commedia*, comm: Christophorus Landinus; *Rime diverse*; Marsilius Ficinus, *Ad Dantem gratulatio*. Ed: Piero da Figino. Venezia: Petrus de Plasiis, Cremonensis, 18 Nov. 1491.

ff. [324]; 2°

ISTC id00033000 (https://data.cerl.org/istc/id00033000)

Bod-Inc Online http://incunables.bodleian.ox.ac.uk/record/D-016

The *editio princeps* (first printed edition) of Dante's lyric poetry includes only his *canzoni* (long lyric poems). It is an appendix to an edition of Cristoforo Landino's commentary on Dante's *Commedia*, one of the seven fifteenth-century reprints of this highly successful commentary that were produced after its publication in 1481.

This edition was printed in Venice on November 18, 1491 by Pietro Cremonese (Pietro Piasi) and was edited by Pietro da Figino, a Franciscan friar, who - unconventionally - signs his edition. The colophon at the end of the *Comentum* indeed reads: "Et fine del *Comento* di Christoforo Landino Fiorentino sopra la *Comedia* di Danthe poeta excellentissimo. E impresso in Vinegia per Petro Cremonese dito Veronese: A dì .xviii. di novembrio M.cccc.Lxxxxi. emendato per me maestro Pietro da Fighino dell'ordine de' frati minori." It is a large *folio*, decorated by 97 small woodcuts, plus three in full page scale, one for each *cantica*. The *canzoni* directly follow the *Commedia* after a blank line. They are printed in three columns, and are introduced by a plain rubric: "Cancione dello excellentissimo poeta Dante Aldigeri fiorentino comminciano qui feliciter." Both copies owned by the Bodleian Library show idiosyncratic interventions by readers (translations and restoration of damaged parts). But none of these interventions pertains to the *canzoni*, and hence we can infer that these readers did not find them interesting.

Copies in the exhibition:

Bodleian Library, Toynbee 1110: damaged copy, restored with manuscript fragments or entire manuscript leaves reproducing the original layout. Images glued from another edition when necessary.

Bodleian Library, Auct. 2 Q inf. 1.43: Copious early marginal and interlinear notes in Spanish (translations of single words or passages from Italian to Spanish). Some notes in Latin.

2. Francesco Petrarca. *Il Petrarcha*. Impresso in Vinegia: Nelle Case D'Aldo Romano, 1514.

184 leaves; 8vo (15cm)

USTC 847800 (https://www.ustc.ac.uk/editions/847800)

In this reprint of Petrarch's *Rerum vulgarium fragmenta* (his lyric collection widely known as the *Canzoniere*) and *Triumphs*, an appendix of various materials has been added to his vernacular poetry by the Venetian printer Aldo Manuzio. The appendix includes three of the poems quoted by Petrarch in his *canzone* 70 "Lasso me" ("Ah me"): Guido Cavalcanti's "Donna me prega" ("A lady asks me"); Cino da Pistoia's "La dolce vista" ("The sweet sight"); and Dante's "Così nel mio parlar vogli' esser aspro" ("I want to be so harsh in my speech"). Added during a second stage of the printing process (the Bodleian holds one of the copies with a shorter appendix, Toynbee 196), it is an example of how printers enticed new customers by adding extras when reprinting an edition. Petrarch was already a best-seller, and so the addition allowed Dante's *canzone* to reach a wider public.

Copies in the exhibition:

Bodleian Library, Auct. 2 R inf. 178 (another copy is held at the Taylorian Library, VET.ITAL.I.A.154)

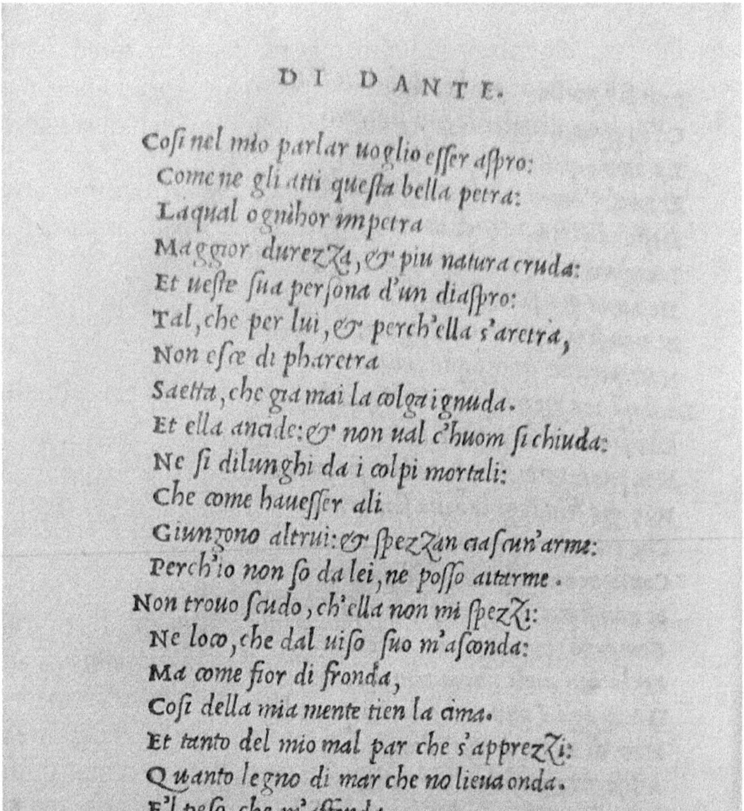

DI DANTE.

Cosi nel mio parlar uoglio esser aspro:
Come ne gli atti questa bella petra:
Laqual ognihor impetra
Maggior durezza, & piu natura cruda:
Et ueste sua persona d'un diaspro:
Tal, che per lui, & perch'ella s'aretra,
Non esce di pharetra
Saetta, che gia mai la colga ignuda.
Et ella ancide: & non ual c'huom si chiuda:
Ne si dilunghi da i colpi mortali:
Che come hauesser ali
Giungono altrui: & spezzan ciascun'arme:
Perch'io non so da lei, ne posso aitarme.
Non trouo scudo, ch'ella non mi spezzi:
Ne loco, che dal uiso suo m'asconda:
Ma come fior di fronda,
Cosi della mia mente tien la cima.
Et tanto del mio mal par che s'apprezzi:
Quanto legno di mar che no lieua onda.
E'l peso, che m'affonda
E' tal, che no'l potrebbe adequar rima.
Ai angosciosa, & dispietata lima,
Che sordamente la mia uita scemi:
Perche non ti ritemi
Si di rodermi 'l cor a scorza a scorza:
Com'io di dir altrui chi ti da forza?

Taylor Inst. Library, VET.ITAL.I.A.154

3. *Sonetti e canzoni di diversi antichi Autori Toscani in dieci libri raccolte. Di Dante Alighieri libri quattro. Di messer Cino da Pistoia libro uno. Di Guido Cavalcanti libro uno. Di Dante da Maiano libro uno. Di fra Guittone d'Arezzo libro uno. Di diverse canzoni e sonetti senza nome d'autore libro uno*. Firenze: Her. di Filippo di Giunta, 1527.

148 leaves; 8°

USTC 800638 (https://www.ustc.ac.uk/editions/800638)

The *editio princeps* (first printed edition) of most 13th- and 14th-century Italian lyric poetry. Containing 289 poems by 23 authors over 11 books, it was designed by Bardo Segni for the Giunta publishing house in Florence.

Dante's lyric poems occupy the first four books, organised into: poems of the *Vita Nuova* (*The New Life*) without any prose (I); other lyric poems, mainly in diverse meters (II); and *canzoni* (long lyric poems, III and IV).

The *Giuntina* corpus has been freed of most of the poems attributed spuriously to Dante which had been circulating. Through selection and organisation, it promoted the reading of Dante's lyric poems as though of a systematic songbook bearing witness to the major steps of his life as a man and a poet.

Copies in the exhibition:

Bodleian Library, Toynbee 425: This copy was owned by Giulio Millo (ownership note on title page), a seventeenth-century Venetian physician, author of the *Naturae morbos decernentis arcanum opus*, 1654 (copy with minor annotations).

Bodleian Library, 8° P 360 Art.: This copy was owned by a Petrus Baldus (copy with minor annotations).

Bodleian Library, Mason FF 158: This copy was decorated with illuminated initials.

Bodleian Library, Mortara 150

4. *Rime di diversi antichi autori toscani in dieci libri raccolte. Di Dante Alighieri libri IIII. Di m. Cino da Pistoia libro I. Di Guido Cavalcanti libro I. Di Dante da Maiano libro I. Di fra Guittone d'Arezzo libro I.* Venezia: Antonio da Sabbio & fratres, 1532.

148 leaves; 8vo

USTC 800773 (https://www.ustc.ac.uk/editions/800773)

An almost identical reprint of the 1527 Florentine Giunti edition. Prepared just five years later in Venice, it shows the success of the selection proposed by Bardo Segni.

Copies in the exhibition:

Bodleian Library, Toynbee 2634

Corpus Christi College Library, Bridges Collection Monographs N15821471: Copy annotated by Robert Seymour Bridges (1844-1930), Poet Laureate from 1913 to 1930.

5. *L'amoroso Conuiuio di Dante, con la additione et molti suoi notandi, accuratamente revisto et emendato.* Venezia: Sessa, 1531.

112 leaves; 8vo

USTC 808776 (https://www.ustc.ac.uk/editions/808776)

This is the fourth printed edition of Dante's *Convivio*. This unfinished work consists of a commentary on Dante's own *canzoni* (long lyric poems), one for each book, and an introductory treatise. He planned to comment on fourteen of his *canzoni*, but he only finished commenting on three of them, and thus we have only four books. The result would have been a vernacular encyclopaedia of philosophy, science, and history. John Donne owned this copy which today is held at the Bodleian. Donne's motto appears on the upper inside wrapper: "Per Rachel ho seruito, & no[n] per Lea." ("I have served Rachel, not Leah;" it is taken from Petrarch's *canzone* 206, referring to *Genesis* 29; it implies that he pursued a contemplative rather than active life). The copy is signed in the bottom right hand corner of the title page: "J: Donne." He left no other annotations or marks on his book. (The title-page is signed in 3 places by Thomas Langton, including at the head of the title displacing Donne's motto.)

Copies in the exhibition:

Bodleian Library, 8° D 19 Art.Seld: copy owned by John Donne.

6. *Vita nuova di Dante Alighieri. Con xv Canzoni del medesimo. E la vita di esso Dante scritta da Giovanni Boccaccio*. Firenze: Sermartelli, 1576.

[8], 116, [6], 3-80 p.; 8vo

USTC 808799 (https://www.ustc.ac.uk/editions/808799)

Dante's lyric poetry did not enjoy the same extensive success of Petrarch's lyric collection, the *Canzoniere*. Nevertheless, Dante's poems were printed five times between 1491 and 1532. His *Vita Nuova* (*The New Life*), on the other hand, had to wait until 1576 to be printed. In this prosimetrum Dante gathered 31 of his poems, accompanying the verse with his own prose commentary. The 1576 Sermartelli edition gathers the *New Life*, the series of 15 *canzoni* (long lyric poems) contained in the manuscript edition of Giovanni Boccaccio (1350s-1360s), and Boccaccio's *Life of Dante*, written to introduce this same edition. Sermartelli based his edition on Florence, Biblioteca Medicea Laurenziana, MS 40.42, and therefore left out the *divisioni*, the technical part of the prose commentary, which was already missing in that source.

Copies in the exhibition:

Taylor Inst. Library: VET.ITAL.I.A.145 Rare N11217057: In Boccaccio's *Life of Dante* there are some reading annotations (crosses in the margins) and a correction.

Bodleian Library 8° X 8 Art.BS.: This copy was owned by Antonio Beffa Negrini (1532-1602), an Italian poet and historian. The 1576 edition of Dante's *Vita Nuova*, *canzoni*, and Boccaccio's *Life of Dante* is bound with a 1583 edition of Gian Giorgio Trissino's translation of Dante's treatise on vernacular language (the *De vulgari eloquentia*) and dialogue on Italian language *Il Castellano*, and with Pierfrancesco Giambullari's *Del sito, forma, et misure, dello Inferno di Dante*. Beffa Negrini signed the editions of Dante and Giambullari. The antique binding and the titles written on the lower edge suggest that the three prints were bound by Antonio himself.

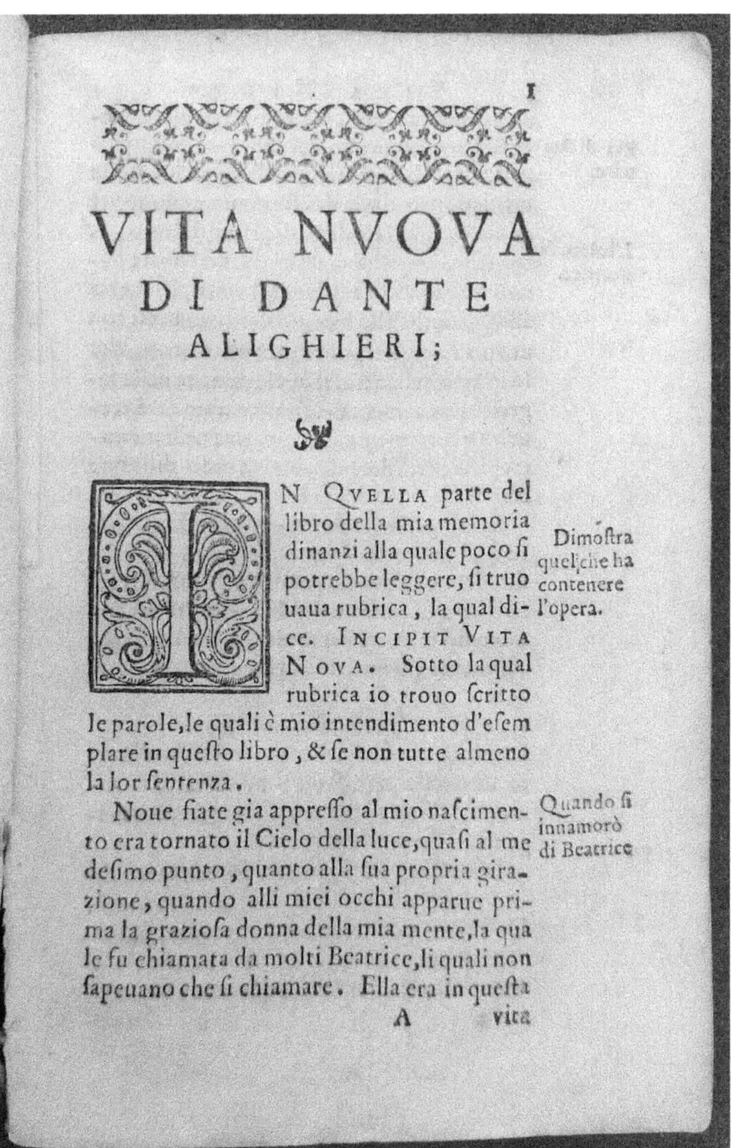

1

VITA NVOVA DI DANTE ALIGHIERI;

IN QVELLA parte del libro della mia memoria dinanzi alla quale poco ſi potrebbe leggere, ſi truouaua rubrica, la qual dice. INCIPIT VITA NOVA. Sotto la qual rubrica io trouo ſcritto le parole, le quali è mio intendimento d'eſemplare in queſto libro, & ſe non tutte almeno la lor ſentenza.

Dimoſtra quel, che ha contenere l'opera.

Noue fiate gia appreſſo al mio naſcimento era tornato il Cielo della luce, quaſi al medeſimo punto, quanto alla ſua propria girazione, quando alli miei occhi apparue prima la grazioſa donna della mia mente, la quale fu chiamata da molti Beatrice, li quali non ſapeuano che ſi chiamare. Ella era in queſta

Quando ſi innamorò di Beatrice

A vita

Taylor Inst. Library, VET.ITAL.I.A.145 Rare N11217057

7. *Sonetti e canzoni di diversi antichi Autori Toscani in dieci libri raccolte*. Firenze: Her. di Filippo di Giunta, 1727. Ed. Afoto Aletino, a spese di Elaumene Loppagi.

298 p.; 12^{0}

During the second half of the sixteenth century and the whole seventeenth century, Dante's lyric poetry was never printed. In 1727 in Florence an editor under the pseudonym of Afoto Aletino (the "unenlightened truthbearer") reprinted the Giuntina to mark its second centenary, inaugurating a series of new editions of Dante's lyric poetry.

The 1727 Giuntina maintains all of the poems encompassed in the 1527 anthology and Bernardo di Giunta's preface. Aletino corrected some errors, improved punctuation and spelling, and added several tools for the reader: another preface, an "avviso al lettore" ("notice to the reader"), an index, and an appendix with variants of Dante's poems. His major intervention, however, was the re-ordering of the poems of the *Vita Nuova* (books I and II): instead of following the order chosen by Dante in his own work, Aletino reorders them by genre.

Copies in the exhibition:

Taylor Inst. Library, VET.ITA.III.A.77 Rare N11644744 >

Bodleian Library, Toynbee 1374

Impreſſo in FIRENZE
a ſpeſe di
ELAUMENE LOPPAGI
Nel meſe di Agoſto
Dell' Anno del SIGNORE
MDCCXXVII.

Modern Editions (19th-20th century)

Laura Banella

From the sixteenth century through to the eighteenth century, Dante's works did not enjoy much success. The *Commedia*, of course, was still widely read, but Dante was not considered to be the foremost Italian author; especially for lyric poetry that, rather, was Petrarch, whose works were read and imitated throughout Europe and beyond. After the first printed edition of his *Vita Nuova* (*The New Life*) in 1576, Dante's lyric poetry was published not even once throughout the whole seventeenth century. Dante came back to prominence in the second part of the eighteenth century, and his renewed fame flourished when in nineteenth-century medievalism and national philology he came to be considered the ethical father of Italian literature and culture. In Britain and especially in England, Dante's popularity experienced sudden and spectacular growth at the end of the eighteenth century. Dante was one of the most popular authors among Romantic writers, and his success did not falter during the Victorian era. In the nineteenth century, Dante's lyric corpus was published many times and, particularly following the Romantic period, was considered as a cohesive songbook. It appeared in several reprints of the 1527 Giuntina anthology of Tuscan poetry, whose first four books contain an already systematized corpus of Dante's lyric poetry, and after 1820 it was included in several anthologies of works by "the most illustrious" Italian poets. The section of the exhibition dedicated to the editions of Dante's lyric poetry spanning the period from the 1820s to the 1930s is but a selection of works from the Taylor Institution Library's vast collection of modern Dantean editions.

The editions of Dante's lyric poetry by Pietro Fraticelli (1834 and 1856, with several reprints of each) soon became widely appreciated and read, and thus their canon of Dante's lyric poems became the most famous. Fraticelli published Dante's lyric poetry in an independent volume within the project of a complete edition of his *opere minori* ("minor works:" that is, Dante's works other than the *Commedia*). The 1834 edition is entitled *Poesie di Dante Alighieri* (*Poems by D.A.*) and collects all the short-form poetry by Dante. Here, the poems are divided by meter –*canzoni, sestine, madrigali, ballate, sonetti*–, including those of the *Vita Nuova* along with the spurious *rime sacre* (or sacred poems, the *Credo* and *Sette salmi*) and the Latin *Egloge*. The texts are preceded by a long and articulated essay on Dante's poetry. Fraticelli's second edition of Dante's poems (1856) is again the first volume in a series of Dante's *opere minori*, and has a lengthy commentary, but its structure is completely different from the first print. The poems are divided into three groups: the *legittime* (legitimate poems), in turn sub-divided into *canzoniere erotico* (erotic songbook) and *canzoniere filosofico* (philosophical songbook); the *dubbie* (uncertain poems); and the *apocrife* (apocryphal poems). This edition by Fraticelli is particularly important because, even though the content has not changed from the 1834 print, it appropriates two innovations that had already appeared in less renowned editions of Dante's poems: 1) it bears the title of *Canzoniere*, "songbook" or "book of poetry," a novelty which had appeared in the 1835 English edition by Charles Lyell (*The Canzoniere of D.A.*), which is the first translation of Dante's lyric poetry into English; 2) it intersperses the poems of the *Vita Nuova* with those considered contemporary – a way of ordering the poems already adopted in a 1839 edition by Le Monnier, when usually poems were ordered by meter, as Fraticelli himself did in 1834. Such a categorisation and ordering of Dante's lyric poetry into overly coherent thematic songbooks does not merely emphasize its ties with the life of the author – it promotes, especially through the concoction of an "erotic songbook", an interpretation of Dante's literary experience as a direct reflection of his life experience. Out of poetic pieces which were written for the most part as independent poems, it creates a new literary work that was never planned by the author of those pieces. The understanding of the lyric genre as a direct mirroring of one's self, which continues to encapsulate what lyric poetry largely still is for us today, became predominant from the beginning of the nineteenth century, with Romanticism. However, this reading is not easily applicable to writings from the Middle Ages, when literature did not carry the same meanings as it does for us today, and poetry was a discipline at the threshold of philosophy and rhetoric.

The symbolic title of *Canzoniere* for Dante's lyric poems was first introduced in Britain. Charles Lyell (1769-1849) was not a professional literary scholar, but he knew and frequented the most important Dante scholars of his time in London. In particular, he became friends with the celebrated and controversial Italian exile Gabriele Rossetti, so much so as to be the godfather of his son, the poet and artist Dante Gabriel Rossetti. In Lyell's "*Canzoniere* di Dante," Gabriele Rossetti is mentioned as an authority on medieval Italian poetry and was supposed to (but ultimately did not) compile a second volume of interpretation of Dante's lyric corpus to accompany Lyell's translations. The translations into English comprise the poems from Dante's *Vita Nuova* and *Convivio*, as well as other scattered poems. Charles Lyell translated all the poems that he found in a previous edition of Dante's lyric poetry, entitled *Amori e rime di Dante Alighieri* (*Loves and Lyrics by D.A.*, Mantua: Caranenti, 1823), curated by Ferdinando Arrivabene. In Arrivabene's edition, as its title suggests, the poems of the *Vita Nuova* and the other lyric poems were ordered and interwoven in order to tell the story of Dante's love for Beatrice, explained in length by Arrivabene. Lyell's translations present the reader "merely with the literal sense of the text; for the allegorical and mystical sense he is referred to the writings of the single commentator who has attempted and hazarded their explanation." Indeed, the translations were supposed to clarify the allegorical-mystical system of interpretation elaborated by Rossetti in order to unveil a (hypothetical) cabalistic *gergo* underpinning "the works of all the Ghibelline writers of that æra." (p. ix) Lyell progressively distanced himself from Rossetti's eccentric interpretations of medieval literature, and in the following reprints (1840, 1842, 1845) his translation of Dante's lyric poetry was issued as an independent volume, without Rossetti's intervention. The title of *Canzoniere* emphasises the comprehensive, Platonic reading that Lyell proposes in his edition, which also includes a summary of Plato's *Symposium*. The Platonic reading of Dante goes back to other nineteenth-century authors and scholars, such as Arthur Hallam and Percy B. Shelley. However, in the 1842 and 1845 reprints, the title is respectively *Poems* and *Lyrical Poems*, echoing Lyell's distancing from Rossetti. The exhibition shows a copy of the first 1835 edition, dedicated by Lyell to Mrs Hooker, the wife of a fellow botanist (another interest that Lyell pursued as a highly skilled amateur).

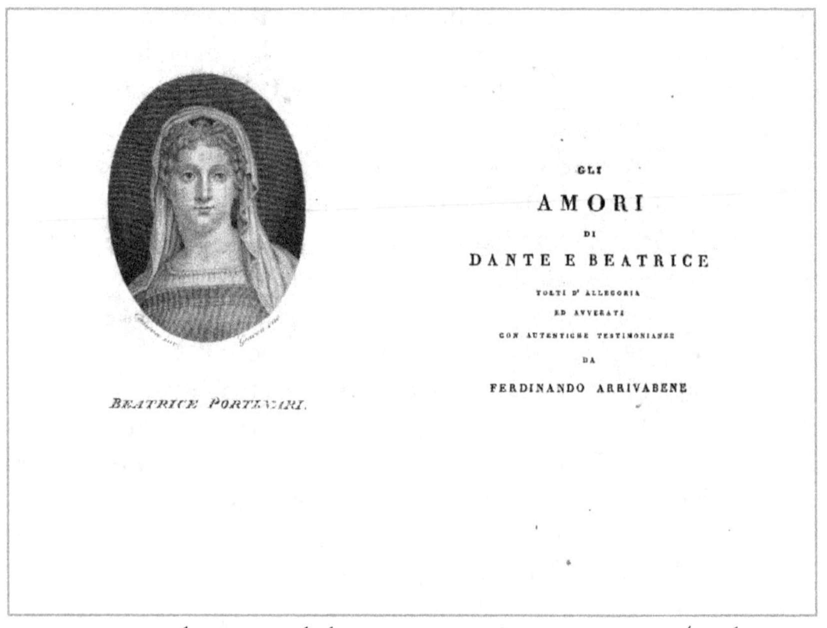

BEATRICE PORTINARI.

GLI

AMORI

DI

DANTE E BEATRICE

TOLTI D' ALLEGORIA

ED AVVERATI

CON AUTENTICHE TESTIMONIANZE

DA

FERDINANDO ARRIVABENE

Amori e rime di Dante Alighieri. Mantua: Caranenti, 1823 (Taylor Inst. Library, VET.ITA.IV.A.69)

Gabriele Rossetti's son, the poet and artist Dante Gabriel (1828-1882), never visited Italy, but his literary and artistic works were deeply affected by Italian language and culture. He was a central figure in the formation of the Pre-Raphaelite Brotherhood, and in Oxford the Ashmolean Museum preserves some of his works. Among these is a watercolour portraying an episode of the *Vita Nuova*: *Dante Drawing an Angel on the Anniversary of Beatrice's Death*. A particularly significant example of Dante Gabriel Rossetti's interest in Dante is his collection and translation into English verse of early Italian poets, which contains Dante's lyric poetry "with the Italian poets preceding him." This exhibition shows the first edition (1861, entitled *The Early Italian Poets from Ciullo d'Alcamo to Dante Alighieri*) and a copy of the second edition of this anthology (1874, expanded and entitled *Dante and His Circle*) owned by Edward Moore, one of the most celebrated Oxonian Dante scholars.

In 1876 Edward Moore, Principal of St Edmund Hall and leading scholar, founded the Oxford Dante Society. He went on to curate the first edition of the whole *oeuvre* of Dante in one single volume: the so-called "Oxford Dante," which was first published in 1894 and then reprinted several times over the following decades. These two enterprises represent the academic pinnacle of the British cult of Dante. The "Oxford Dante" is divided into two parts: works in verse and in prose. It is opened by the *Commedia*, followed by Dante's lyric poetry, again under the title of *Canzoniere*, and then there are the *Egloge* and the spurious poems (*Credo* and *Sette salmi*). The second section, dedicated to prose works, consists of *Vita Nuova*, *Convivio*, *Monarchia*, *De Vulgari Eloquentia*, *Epistolae* and *Questio de Aqua et Terra*. This edition is completely in Italian, including the editor's introduction, in which Moore states that they had purposely created a "volume portatile, e quasi tascabile," ("a portable volume, and almost pocket-sized"). Dante's lyric poems were corrected and organized by the *valente Dantofilo* York Powell, a member of the Oxford Dante Society who promoted the publication of the "Oxford Dante." Dante's *canzoniere* is divided into four sections: *§I. Poesie della Vita nuova (Poems of the V.N.)*; *§II. Poesie del Convivio (Poems of the C.)*; *§III. Poesie citate nel Trattato De Vulgari Eloquentia (Poems cited in the Treatise De Vulgari Eloquentia)*; *§IV. Poesie che non si trovano citate in nessuna opera del Poeta (Poems that are not cited in any work of the Poet)*. While mentioned in this index, the poems of the *Vita Nuova* and of the *Convivio* are printed within the prosimetra in the second part of the volume. In the last section, which contains most of the corpus, the poems are ordered by meter –*sestine, canzoni, sonetti, ballate*– and then alphabetically within each section. This edition encapsulates how the perception of Dante's lyric poetry evolved during the nineteenth century. In particular it emphasizes one of the features that had already been adopted by Fraticelli in 1856, to which Moore explicitly refers for the text: that is, the use of the title *Canzoniere*, first introduced by Lyell. At the same time, the inclusion of the poems of the *Vita Nuova* and of the *Convivio* is only stated in the index, while the lyrics stay in their place. Moreover, ordering the poems by meter and then alphabetically is far from the idea of a songbook. This is a completely different editorial solution from what had been done before; it is also different from how the corpus was subsequently crystallized. During the nineteenth century, Dante's lyric poems were progressively perceived as a systematic songbook, and thus edited as a *Canzoniere*: a book of poetry which to varying extents might also include the poems from the prosimetra and – especially – those of the *Vita Nuova*. Hence, Dante's lyric production was taken to show his development as a lyric writer and to exhibit the stages of his literary career, leading inexorably to the masterpiece, the *Commedia*. In the "Oxford Dante" the lyric poems are entitled *Canzoniere* and a table recapitulates the structure of the supposed songbook by Dante; the poems, however, are either within the prosimetra, or impersonally ordered. The Taylor Institution Library holds several copies of the "Oxford Dante," some of which belonged to Moore and bear his autograph notes (the notes mostly relate to typographical errors to be corrected in further editions of the volume). Likewise, some of these volumes owned by Moore contain various loose sheets with further corrections, and other notes relating to Dante and his works and to the Oxford Dante Society.

The indices of the "Oxford Dante" were prepared by Paget Toynbee, the celebrated Oxonian Dante scholar who would make considerable contributions to the collections of Oxford libraries in the form of modern and antique books, some of which are part of this exhibition (indeed their shelfmark is Toynbee). Among the many excellent works by Toynbee, the exhibition shows a copy of his *Dictionary of Proper Names and Notable Matters in the Works of Dante* (Oxford University Press, 1897), which also contains an index of the first lines of the *Canzoniere*. The first "Index of Proper Names in the Prose Works and *Canzoniere* of Dante" (which was later fused with the *Dictionary*) had already been published by Toynbee in 1894 in the *Annual Reports of the Dante Society* (No 13, pp. 3-28).

In 1921 the Società Dantesca Italiana curated an edition of Dante's *oeuvre* to celebrate the sixth-hundredth anniversary of Alighieri's death. This edition of the whole corpus of Dante's works is contained in one single volume, just like the "Oxford Dante." The edition of the lyric poems – entitled *Rime* (*Poems*) – and of the *Vita Nuova* is curated by Michele Barbi, who edited the volume as well. Here, Dante's lyric poems are set between the *Vita Nuova* and the *Convivio* and divided in seven *libri* ("books"), established through chronological and thematic criteria, each one with a meaningful title. The first line of each poem of the *Vita Nuova* is recalled, thus creating a mosaic with all of Dante's poems that is inspired by a tradition going back to the 1527 Giuntina.

In 1939 Gianfranco Contini published for Einaudi the first modern, commented, scholarly edition of Dante's lyric poetry, entitled *Rime* (*Poems*). Contini excluded the poems from the *Vita Nuova* and the *Convivio*. Furthermore, as he began his introduction by distancing himself from Lyell's title of *Canzoniere* and the perspective it embodied, Contini showed himself eager to emphasise that Dante's lyric poems were "the most magnificent collection of scattered poems." While Michele Barbi's systematic placement of the poems in a meaningful series implicitly leads to an understanding of Dante's production as a "life songbook," Contini underscores the independence of the corpus from any idea of a *Canzoniere*. At the same time, it was Barbi who abandoned the term *Canzoniere* (which he used through his 1915 *Studi sul Canzoniere di Dante*) for the more neutral *Rime*, and who in this same 1921 edition did not treat the poems as an independent section of Dante's literary *oeuvre*.

By freeing the corpus from unnecessary biographical over-interpretations, both Barbi and Contini brought Dante's lyric poetry into modernity. Nevertheless, editions of Dante's lyric poems continued to be printed that were based on an often too simplistic biographical interpretation of his lyric poetry. As an example of this kind of interpretation, the exhibition displays a copy of Giuseppe Zonta's 1925 edition of Dante's lyric poetry. Here, each poem is placed into an overly coherent narrative arc, strengthened by the editor's introductions, while illustrations give the impression of a tormented romance. Thus Zonta interprets according to a contemporary framework the desire and passion expressed by Dante in his lyric poetry, when this mode of expression should rather be evaluated within not only its medieval context, but also Dante's multifaceted literary and philosophical engagement, already present in his early lyric works.

The Selection of Modern Editions of Dante's Lyric Poetry in the Exhibition

Narrating Dante's Life and Love Through His Lyric Poetry

Amori e rime di Dante Alighieri. Mantua: Caranenti, 1823.

The Canzoniere of Dante Alighieri including the Poems of the 'Vita Nuova' and 'Convito': Italian and English, trans. by Charles Lyell. London: John Murray, 1835.

Poesie di Dante Alighieri precedute da un discorso intorno alla loro legittimità, a cura di Pietro Fraticelli. Florence: Allegrini e Mazzoni, 1834.

Il Canzoniere di Dante Alighieri, annotato e illustrato da Pietro Fraticelli aggiuntovi le rime sacre e le poesie latine dello stesso autore. Florence: Barbèra e Bianchi, 1856.

Dante's Canzoniere in Britain

Canzoni e sonetti di Dante Alighieri, per la prima volta di note illustrate da Romualdo Zotti. London: Zotti, 1809.

Dante Gabriel Rossetti, and Dante Alighieri. *The Early Italian Poets from Ciullo D'Alcamo to Dante Alighieri (1100-1200-1300) : In the Original Metres, Together with Dante's Vita Nuova*. London: Smith Elder, 1861.

Dante Gabriel Rossetti, and Dante Alighieri. *Dante and His Circle : With the Italian Poets Preceding Him (1100-1200-1300) : A Collection of Lyrics*. Rev. and Re-arranged ed. London: Ellis and White, 1874.

"Tutto Dante"

Dante Alighieri, *Tutte le Opere*, ed. Edward Moore. Oxford: Oxford UP, 1894 [1st ed.]

Dante Alighieri, *Le opere: testo critico della Società dantesca italiana*, a cura di Michele Barbi et al. Florence: Bemporad, 1921.

Different "Dantes" for the 20th Century

Dante Alighieri, *Canzoniere*, a cura di Giuseppe Zonta. Turin: Paravia, 1923.

Dante Alighieri, *Rime*, ed. Gianfranco Contini. Turin: Einaudi, 1939 [1946 2nd ed.]

Loose leaf from Taylor Inst. Library, Moore I b 14 a

Drawing of the Church of Saint Sevérin in Paris.

"Dante | Rue du Fouarre. Paris"

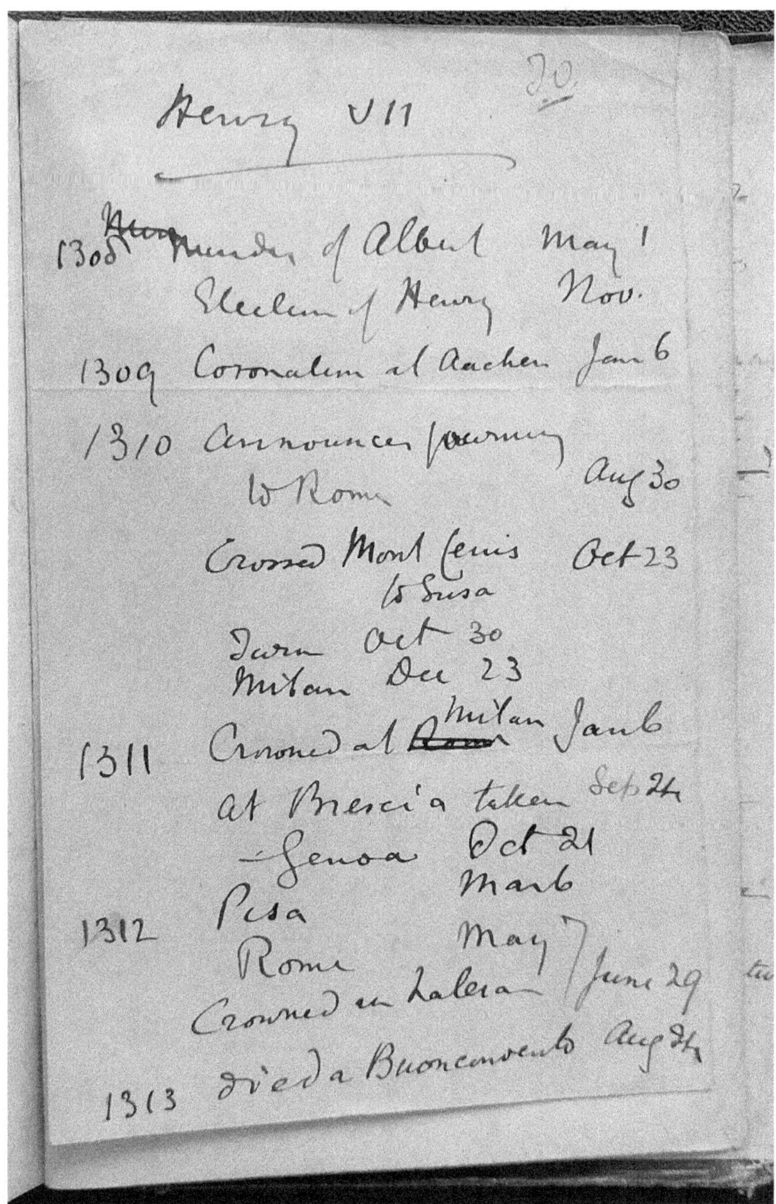

Henry VII 30

1308 Murder of Albert May 1
Election of Henry Nov.
1309 Coronation at Aachen Jan 6
1310 Announces journey to Rome Aug 30
Crossed Mont Cenis to Susa Oct 23
Turin Oct 30
Milan Dec 23
1311 Crowned at Milan Jan 6
at Brescia taken Sep 24
Genoa Oct 21
Pisa Mar 6
1312 Rome May 7
Crowned in Lateran June 29
1313 died a Buonconvento Aug 24

Loose leaf from Taylor Inst. Library, Moore I b 12

Dates related to Henry VII's descent to Italy (1308-1313)

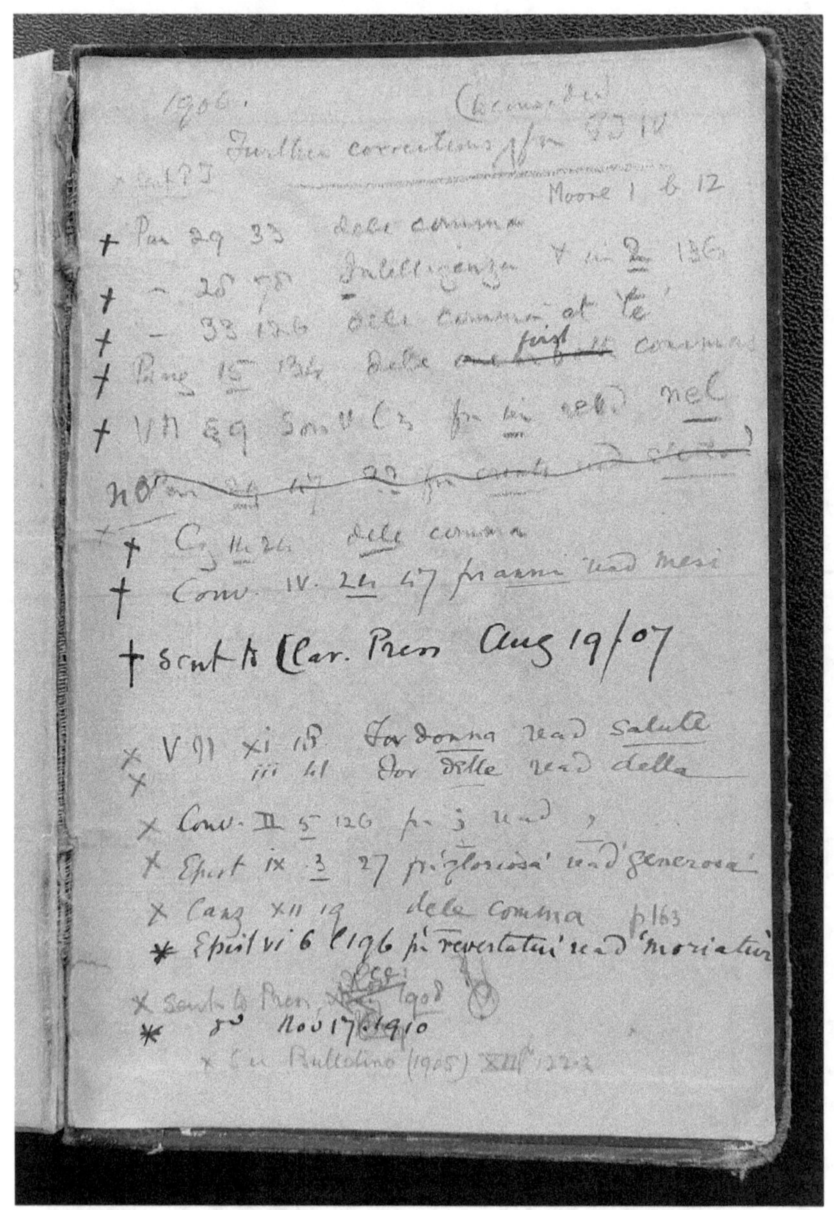

1906.

Further corrections

Moore I b 12

+ Par 29 33 dele comma

+ – 33 126 dele comma at 'te'

+ Purg 15 136 dele first comma

+ Conv. IV. 24 47 for anni read mesi

+ sent to Clar. Press Aug 19/07

x V N xi 18 for donna read salute

x iii 41 for delle read della

x Conv. II 5 126

x Epist ix 3 27 for 'gloriosa' read 'generosa'

x Canz XII 19 dele comma p163

* Epist vi 6 l 196 for 'revertatur' read 'moriatur'

x Sent to Press 1908

* do Nov 17 1910

Taylor Inst. Library, Moore I b 12

List of typographical errors to be corrected in a further edition

Essential Bibliography

Alighieri, Dante. *Convivio,* ed. Franca Brambilla Ageno. Florence: Le Lettere, 1995.

---. *La Vita Nuova*, ed. Michele Barbi. Florence: Bemporad, 1932.

---. *Rime*, ed. Domenico De Robertis. Florence: Le Lettere, 2002.

---. *Il Convivio (The Banquet)*, trans. Richard H. Lansing. Garland Library of Medieval Literature, Ser. B. N, New York: Garland, 1990.

---. *De Vulgari Eloquentia*, ed. and transl. Steven Botterill. Cambridge: Cambridge University Press, 1996.

Dante's Lyric Poetry, eds. Patrick Boyde, and Kenelm Foster,2 vols.. Oxford: Oxford UP, 1967.

Dante's Lyric Poetry: Poems of Youth and of the 'Vita Nuova', eds. Teodolinda Barolini, trans. Richard Lansing. Toronto-Buffalo-London: University of Toronto Press, 2014.

Montale, Eugenio. *Collected Poems 1920-1954*, transl. and notes by Jonathan Galassi. New York: Farrar, Straus and Giroux, 1998.

Petrarch's Lyric Poems. The Rime sparse *and Other Lyrics*, trans. and ed. Robert M. Durling. Cambridge-London: Harvard University Press, 1976.

Ascoli, Albert Russell. *Dante and the Making of a Modern Author*. Cambridge: Cambridge University Press, 2008.

Banella, Laura. "The Fortunes of an "Authorial" Edition: Boccaccio's *Vita nuova* in Antonio Pucci and il Saviozzo," in *Boccaccio 1313 – 2013*, eds. F. Ciabattoni, E. Filosa, K. Olson, Ravenna: Longo, 2015, 237-48.

---. "The 'Dante Canon': Collecting Dante's Lyric Poetry in the Fourteenth Century," *Dante Studies* 134 (2016): 169-94.

---. "The Lyric Dante in the Twentieth Century: Hermeneutics and Editorial Forms." *Italian Studies* 75/3 (2020): 307-25.

Barański, Zygmunt G. "Dante and Montale," in *Dante Comparisons. Comparative Studies of Dante and: Montale, Foscolo, Tasso, Chaucer, Petrarch,*

Propertius and Catullus, eds. Eric Haywood, Barry Jones. Dublin: Irish Academic Press, 1985, 11-48.

---. *Dante, Petrarch, Boccaccio: Literature, Doctrine, Reality.* Cambridge: Legenda – Modern Humanities Research Association, 2020.

Barolini, Teodolinda. *Dante and the Origins of Italian Literary Culture*. New York: Fordham University Press, 2006.

Dante in the Long Nineteenth Century, eds. Aida Audeh and Nick Havely. Oxford: Oxford University Press, 2012.

Daniels, Rhiannon. *Boccaccio and the Book: Production and Reading in Italy 1340-1520*. London: Legenda, 2009.

Durling, Robert M., Ronald L. Martinez. *Time and the Crystal : Studies in Dante's Rime Petrose*. Berkeley- Los Angeles-Oxford: University of California Press, 1990.

Eisner, Martin. *Boccaccio and the Invention of Italian Literature: Dante, Petrarch, Cavalcanti, and the Authority of the Vernacular*. Cambridge-New York: Cambridge University Press, 2013.

---. *Dante's New Life of the Book: A Philology of World Literature*. Oxford: Oxford University Press, 2021.

Gilson, Simon. *Dante and Renaissance Florence*. Cambridge: Cambridge University Press, 2005.

---. *Reading Dante in Renaissance Italy. Florence, Venice and the 'Divine Poet'*. Cambridge: Cambridge University Press, 2018.

Havely, Nick. *Dante's British Public: Readers and Texts, from the Fourteenth Century to the Present*. Oxford: Oxford University Press, 2014.

Italy's Three Crowns: Reading Dante, Petrarch and Boccaccio, eds. Zygmunt G. Barański and Martin L. McLaughlin. Oxford: Bodleian Library, 2007.

Parker, Deborah. *Commentary and Ideology : Dante in the Renaissance*. Durham-London: Duke University Press, 1993.

www.ingramcontent.com/pod-product-compliance
Lightning Source LLC
Chambersburg PA
CBHW071014120726
47910CB00004B/1516

* 9 7 8 0 9 9 5 4 5 6 4 7 1 *